YELLOWSTONE

A PICTURE MEMORY

Text
Bill Harris

Editorial
David Gibbon

Captions
Nicola Dent

Production
Ruth Arthur
Sally Connolly
Neil Randles
Andrew Whitelaw

Design
Teddy Hartshorn

Photography
Colour Library Books Ltd.

Director of Production
Gerald Hughes

Commissioning Editor
Andrew Preston

CLB 2869
© 1992 Colour Library Books Ltd., Godalming, Surrey, England
All rights reserved
This 1992 edition published by Crescent Books,
distributed by Outlet Book Company, Inc., a Random House Company,
40 Engelhard Avenue, Avenel, New Jersey 07001
Color separations by Scantrans Pte Ltd., Singapore
Printed and bound in Singapore
ISBN 0 517 07268 8
8 7 6 5 4 3 2 1

YELLOWSTONE

A PICTURE MEMORY

CRESCENT BOOKS
NEW YORK · AVENEL, NEW JERSEY

There are dozens of names on the Yellowstone landscape that immortalize explorers and trappers and others who opened our eyes to the wonders of the Rocky Mountain wilderness. But there is no famous landmark dedicated to the memory of Cornelius Hedges. None, that is, except Yellowstone National Park itself. It was his idea.

The thought took shape on a starry September night in 1870, quite appropriately over a roaring campfire on the banks of the steaming Firehole River. The men around the fire had spent the summer exploring the area and, as they were getting ready to go back to civilization, their conversation naturally turned to the incredible things they had seen. They discussed what God had created there and talked about what might happen when man came along to improve on it. The consensus among them was that the territory ought to be put under government control for orderly speculation. But Cornelius Hedges had a better idea. What if the government set it aside for the use of all the people, with no restrictions other than that it remain unchanged and undeveloped?

It was a revolutionary idea, to be sure, and considering the long-standing history of land speculation that had become part of the American experience and a key to the opening of the West, it also had all the earmarks of an impossible dream. But Hedges convinced his fellow explorers that it was an idea worth fighting for, and he himself started the ball rolling with an article published in the Helena, Montana, *Herald*. Another member of the party, Nathaniel P. Langford, went on a lecture tour that included stops in Chicago, Washington and New York, and his message moved an editorial writer for the *New York Herald* to tell his readers that "...this new field of wonders should at once be withdrawn from occupancy and set apart as a public national park for the enjoyment of the American people for all time."

He was the first to use the term "national park," and on March 1, 1872, it became part of the language when President Ulysses S. Grant signed the bill that made Yellowstone the world's first national park.

Nathaniel Langford, who became the first superintendent of the new park, and Cornelius Hedges were part of a nine-man expedition headed by Henry D. Washburn, the Surveyor General of Montana, that went into the wilderness accompanied by a military escort of four soldiers commanded by Lieutenant Gustavus C. Doane. Ironically, their mission was intended to prove that the reports made by a previous exploration were pure fantasy. One of them wrote: "I think a more confirmed set of skeptics never went out into the wilderness than those who composed our party, and never was a party more completely surprised and captivated with the wonders of nature." They weren't alone in their skepticism. The previous expedition had itself been organized to put to rest the wild tales of mountain men who described steaming rivers, bubbling mud and towering geysers. And even when they saw such things for themselves they didn't think anyone would believe them, either.

The three men, David E. Folsom, C.W. Cook and William Peterson, entered the present limits of the park in 1869 near today's North Entrance at Gardiner, Montana. In their 36-day trip, they discovered the falls of the Yellowstone River as well as its spectacular Grand Canyon. They trekked through Hayden Valley, passed the Sulphur Caldron and the Mud Volcano and explored the west shore of Yellowstone Lake. They went from there to Shoshone Lake and then headed north through the Geyser Basin. It was enough to convince anyone that the trappers who had described these things weren't crazy after all, but when they got back they began to worry that they, too, might be regarded as crazy. According to one report, "they were unwilling to risk their reputations for veracity by a full recital to a small company whom their friends had assembled to hear the account of their explorations."

But David Folsom decided to take the risk. He wrote an article about Yellowstone for *Western Monthly Magazine* and, as strange as the story seemed to be, his readers were willing to believe it and the stage was set for the Washburn Expedition to prove it was all quite true.

But even they weren't quite prepared for what they saw. When they came to the Tower Fall, they were so impressed that they lingered for two full days admiring the 132-foot cataract and the rock formations around it. Even the military man, Doane, couldn't contain his enthusiasm when he wrote, "nothing can be more chastely beautiful than this lovely cascade, hidden away in the dim light of overshadowing rocks and woods, its very voice hushed to a low murmur, unheard at a distance of a few hundred yards."

Like Adam and Eve in the Garden of Eden, they flitted from place to place, giving names to everything they saw. They came up with the name for Tower Fall because the canyon below looked to them like "some old castle." They were less romantic about the individual rock formations, one of which they named Devil's Hoof, and a group above the Fall looked to them like the Devil's Den. When they found Washburn Hot Springs, which later explorers named for their leader, they named them Hell Broth Springs.

Even before they reached the Grand Canyon of the Yellowstone, they were stunned by the river's Black Canyon, which Doane said had taken their breath away. His diary tells us, "standing on the brink of the chasm, the heavy roaring of the imprisoned river comes to the ear in a sort of hollow-hungry growl, scarcely audible from the depths and strongly suggestive of demons in torment below. ... [It is] grand, gloomy and terrible, an empire of shadows and turmoil."

But there was much more to this grand empire than gloom, shadows and turmoil, and they found out how much more when they climbed to the top of the 3,122-foot Mount Washburn. What they saw from there was Yellowstone Lake with the river flowing north from it, and, of course, the Grand Canyon stretching 20 miles into the distance. Although they felt free to name everything else they saw, the river already had a name.

The Indians called it Yellowstone, and trappers had long-since appropriated the designation because they, too, were impressed by the color of the lava transformed by the chemical reaction of super-hot, underground minerals. The Washburn party didn't know why the canyon walls were brilliant shades of yellow and red, and they didn't know that melting snow makes them even more vivid in the spring. But even in the dry season the canyon was so beautiful that one of them said he "stayed two hours in one spot and drank in inspiration." They all stayed in the canyon for more than a day, admiring the waterfall, inspecting the rocks and congratulating one another that they were the first white men ever to walk there.

A few days after exploring the Mud Volcano area and remarking that it made noises "like the bursting of heavy guns," they followed the trail of the earlier explorers around Yellowstone Lake. It was there that disaster struck. One of the men, Truman Evarts, got separated from the rest of the party and, after a few days of searching, they gave him up for dead. The hunt was hindered by an 18-inch snowfall – even though it was mid-September – which was a signal to the others that if they expected to get out alive themselves it was time to get a move on.

It was bitter cold, their feet were wet, their horses dragging. They were depressed about the fate of poor Evarts and even the quiet beauty of the thick pine forest seemed more oppressive than inspiring.

Then, all of a sudden, they came upon a wonder the like of which none of them had ever seen before. Ahead of them in an open valley, a jet of steam and water was rising at least 150 feet into the air and the plume of steam was caught by the breeze, which spread it like a curtain across the valley floor.

"We spurred our jaded horses," said one, "to gather around this wonderful phenomenon." It didn't take them long to give the phenomenon a name. After spending a day in the area, they noticed that they could almost set their watches by the geyser's activity, and that suggested their name for it: Old Faithful.

Back then the geyser erupted almost exactly every 65 minutes. But earthquakes in 1959 and again in 1983 have made it a little less reliable. Now it comes roaring out of the ground every 69 to 76 minutes. Not quite as faithful as before, but still spectacular, each eruption lasts about four minutes, sending some 10,000 gallons of scalding water 150 feet into the air.

Spectacular as it is, Old Faithful isn't the biggest of the Yellowstone geysers. Before the Washburn Party left the Upper Geyser Basin they discovered seven more, including the one they named the Giant, the highest in the world, erupting every ten days to two weeks as much as 250 feet into the air and continuing for as long as an hour and a half. They named the Giantess, too, and she gushes almost 200 feet, but only a few times a year. There are dozens of others Washburn's men overlooked among the 143 geysers in the Basin, ranging from the Anemone, that spits a few feet into the air for about 30 seconds at a time, to the Catfish that rises about eight feet all the time. But they had obviously seen enough, and when they began publishing articles about the Yellowstone area people began to believe it really existed. Until then it had been simply too incredible to comprehend.

In the meantime, the lost Truman Evarts found his way back to civilization on his own and the tales he told made the best reading of all. It isn't easy even now to track through the thick woodlands of Yellowstone without marked trails to follow. But it was doubly tough for the 54-year-old Evarts, who was nearsighted and had broken his glasses. When he wanted to examine a trail, he had to get down on his knees to do it. Fortunately, however, he had a small pair of binoculars, which not only helped him find his way but made it easy for him to build fires when the sun was shining. But he didn't have a gun to provide food, and his horse wandered off on the second day of his month-long ordeal. After he was rescued he moved back east to New York, but no one missed him in Montana. When he wasn't wandering in the woods Truman Evarts was the Territory's tax collector.

The articles and lectures by members of the Washburn Party became the most fascinating topic of conversation across America since the return of the Lewis and Clark Expedition six decades earlier. Official Washington took note, and to help make their decision on the growing enthusiasm for the creation of a national park, they announced not one, but two more expeditions down the Yellowstone River. One of them, led by geologist Ferdinand V. Hayden, included the photographer William Henry Jackson, whose images finally proved once and for all that the unbelievable stories about the place were quite true. But neither the Hayden Expedition nor the military group led by Colonel John W. Barlow covered much new ground. Among the discoveries they made were Mammoth Hot Springs, which Hayden called White Mountain Hot Springs and Barlow noted on his maps as Soda Mountain. Both groups followed the Specimen Ridge Trail and found the Petrified Forest near the base of Amethyst Mountain.

The military expedition wasn't taken very seriously because it was well known that members of the peacetime army were especially fond of two-hour lunches and not much else. It was also noted that Colonel Barlow carried an umbrella to protect himself from the sun, and about all anyone could say about his second in command, Captain David P. Heap, was that he was "a small man." But, in addition to photographers of its own, the Barlow group also had artists along, and between them the two expeditions made five maps of the country they explored. The maps weren't too accurate, but the photographs and sketches were dramatic enough to help Washington get the picture, and it took about five months for Congress to put its stamp of approval on the idea that was born around a campfire less than two years earlier.

It was an incredibly short space of time for any U.S. Congress to act on any idea, least of all one with such far-reaching implications. But the idea of creating a national park was an incredible one, and it was helped along by the veterans of the Washburn Expedition, who hardly missed a beat in their lobbying efforts. Each of them made frequent trips to Washington and all of them made sure that every Congressman and Senator got a copy of every magazine and newspaper article written about the Yellowstone area. They wrote many of them themselves and encouraged others to follow their lead. They also enlisted the services of Montana's Territorial Delegate to Congress, William H. Clagett, to introduce the National Park Bill and to work for its passage. We all owe them a great debt. And so do our grandchildren.

Yellowstone is still the biggest national park in the 48 contiguous states, covering more than two million acres. Seven national forests and three national wildlife refuges around it preserve another eight million acres and Grand Teton National Park to its south adds yet another three hundred thousand; all of which give Americans a virtually unspoiled wilderness bigger than the country of Switzerland. But the statistics about Yellowstone all by itself are astounding. There are 165 streams, most of them alive with trout and all of them with lively waterfalls and rapids. There are 36 lakes and mountain peaks, as well as canyons and flower-strewn hillsides at every turn. The animal population is equally incredible, ranging from meadow mice to moose. There are herds of bison, packs of coyotes, bands of bighorn sheep and pronghorn antelope, and it often seems as though there is an elk behind every tree. In the fall, eagles fly in to feed on the salmon that have made the same trip the hard way. They often compete with ospreys for the same morsels, and thousands of ducks carefully stay out of the way of both. There are swans and cranes, even seagulls and pelicans, on the lakes. There are hawks and hummingbirds and herons and, forever changing the landscape, incredibly busy beavers. But in spite of the abundance of wildlife that is to be seen, the most often-asked question at any of the Park's visitor centers is "Where can I see the bears?"

It is a question visitors began asking the day the Park opened, but bear-watching became synonymous with Yellowstone back in the 1920s, when a big black bear decided to take a noonday nap in the middle of one of the roads that describes a great figure eight in the heart of the of the Park. A tour bus came along, but no amount of horn-blowing could make the bear get out of the way, and he didn't move until one of the passengers tossed a ham sandwich out of the window. The bear gulped it down and let the bus pass, but the following day it was back in the same spot, and once again it wouldn't move until someone tossed food in its direction.

The bear must have had a bus schedule tacked to the wall of its den, because every time a tour passed, there it was waiting to be fed. In time it became the highlight of touring Yellowstone by bus, and drivers, who began calling the bear "Jesse James," could almost guarantee that their passengers would be "held up" along the way. As fast as word spread among visitors, it seemed to spread among the bears as well, and the begging bears of Yellowstone became as famous as Old Faithful and an even bigger tourist attraction.

There is a good reason for it. Bears are fun to watch. They're playful looking and cuddly cute, and it's a rare American of any age whose best friend at some point wasn't a Teddy bear. In the peaceful environment of Yellowstone it's easy to forget that they are wild animals, with lightning-fast reflexes and enough strength easily to chew off the hand extended to feed them. Strong warnings and strictly-enforced laws have reduced the number of injuries over the years, but there are still a few people every year who don't listen to the warnings and break the law. There was a time not too long ago when bears who injured humans were shot, but today they are captured and moved deep into the wilderness where tourists rarely go. The offending animal is marked, and if it should wander back to its home territory it is removed again, and if it comes back a third time it is quietly destroyed.

It is a rare experience, and quite a treat, to see a bear along a Yellowstone roadside today, and if one should happen to wander into the areas popular with human visitors it will probably be a black bear and not a grizzly, its much bigger cousin. Park rangers estimate there are about 200 grizzlies in Yellowstone, but you have to take their word for it because they are as standoffish as black bears are irrepressible, and are almost never seen except in the back country.

But if it isn't possible to tell anyone where to see the bears, there is much more to Yellowstone than wildlife and wilderness. The Algonquin Indians of the East Coast told stories of young braves who searched for God and heaven itself by traveling west and finding both in a mysteriously beautiful mountain. The place they had in mind could easily have been Yellowstone. No one can come away from it without having experienced a deep emotion about it, and very few can find the right words to describe how they feel.

West Thumb Geyser Basin, on the shores of Yellowstone Lake, is a small, concentrated thermal area of geysers and hot springs. One of the most beautiful features is brilliant blue Abyss Pool (facing page).

Minerva Terrace (below, facing page top and bottom, and overleaf) and White Elephant Back Terrace (facing page center) are located in Yellowstone's famous Mammoth Hot Springs. Both consist of ornate, terrace-like formations made of travertine, a form of calcium carbonate dissolved from limestone and carried to the surface by the hot water. Up to two feet of new travertine are deposited annually and as a result the "steps" continually change. The older terraces are pure white in color, while the delicate tints on the newer ones are due to microscopic bacteria and algae mats.

14

Norris Geyser Basin has many exciting thermal features within a two-mile walk. These include Crackline Lake (right) and Nuphar Lake (bottom right). In the northern half of the basin the gray-white geyserite of Porcelain Basin (overleaf) can be crossed via a boardwalk. Above right: this lake near Roaring Mountain, now tranquil, once echoed to the roar of nearby fumeroles. Above: Great Fountain Geyser, Firehole Lake Drive. Facing page top: Spasm Geyser and bubbling mud springs (facing page bottom), found on Fountain Paint Pot Nature Trail. Below: the 40-foot Firehole Falls.

These pages: located on the Firehole River, Midway Geyser Basin is the site of some of the largest hot springs in the world. The two main features of this area are Grand Prismatic Spring (facing page), Yellowstone's largest spring, and Excelsior Geyser, once the most powerful in the Park. In September 1985, Excelsior erupted for the first time since 1888. Despite its inactivity, over 5 million gallons of boiling water still churn daily from its gigantic crater and cascade down runoff channels to warm the waters of the Firehole River (left). As a result of this and other thermal runoff, the river does not freeze in winter and attracts birds, bison and elk to its banks.

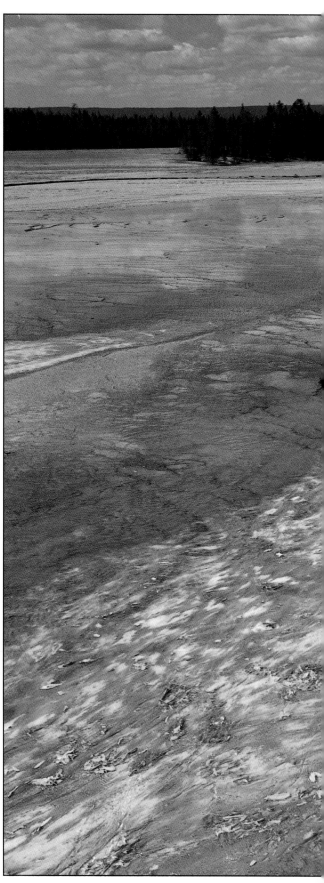

Grand Prismatic Spring at Midway Geyser Basin (these pages and overleaf) can be easily reached by a boardwalk, which skirts around the edge of the crater. Not only memorable for its size, being 370 feet in diameter, this spring is also spectacular for its brilliant colors. The deep blue of the pool contrasts with great rings of vivid orange and yellow algae and bacteria that thrive in the warm thermal waters. A blue haze rises several feet above the pool and combines with the orange and yellow hues to give the effect of a giant prism, hence the name of this spring. Facing page bottom: Flood Geyser Group, Midway Geyser Basin.

Upper Geyser Basin (these pages) has the largest concentration of geysers in the world. Above: Castle Geyser and (top right), Grand Geyser, the highest predictable geyser still active. Most erratic are Spasmodic Geyser (bottom right) and those in the Daisy Geyser Group (facing page top), capable of erupting unexpectedly. Below and facing page bottom: Old Faithful, probably the world's most well-known geyser, is appropriately named as its thermal patterns have altered little in over a century. Right: fantastic shapes of geyserite-covered trees at Grotto Geyser. Overleaf: the Firehole River.

Facing page top: Castle Geyser, thought to be the oldest in Yellowstone, has the largest cone – 120 feet in circumference – made up of gray, rock-like geyserite deposits. Facing page center and overleaf: beautiful Morning Glory Pool, named for its resemblance in shape and color to the morning glory flower. The area around Grotto Geyser is touched with a distinctive red (facing page bottom). According to legend, the Firehole River (below) flows so fast that the friction between it and the riverbed heats the water, but in reality its waters are warmed by runoff from hot springs in the Midway Geyser Basin.

Over 70 percent of visitors come to Yellowstone in July and August, but many enjoy visiting during the winter months when the Park becomes even more magical. Bison grazing at Midway Geyser Basin (below) and at Black Sand Basin (facing page top) are well prepared for the winter months with their heavy, woolly coats. Facing page center: Porcelain Basin and its geysers seem almost more spectacular during winter when the scalding steam meets icy air. Facing page bottom: winter scene at Lower Geyser Basin. Overleaf: viewed from Artist's Point, the Lower Falls of the Yellowstone River drop an incredible 308 feet.

Black Sand Basin (these pages) has some of the most beautiful thermal scenery in the Park. Colors from the surrounding area are reflected in Opalescent Pool (bottom right, facing page and overleaf), and the stark, twisted outlines of dead trees rise from its shores. Emerald Pool (top right) is remarkable for its translucent green center fringed by orange and yellow algae. Above: Steamboat Geyser, the most powerful geyser in Yellowstone, erupts to heights of 300-350 feet. Below: Echinus Geyser, which spouts every 40-70 minutes. Right: Cistern Spring.

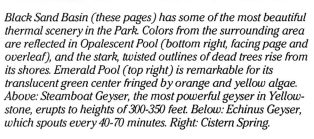

These pages: West Thumb Geyser Basin, on the edge of Yellowstone Lake (facing page top and overleaf), is a small thermal area of hot springs and geysers. Its most spectacular features include the brilliant blue Abyss Pool (bottom left) and the Percolating Springs (below). Left, top left and above: water seeps underground, is heated by the lava or magma of the earth, then surfaces as a geyser or, as here, in the form of hot springs. Facing page bottom: at Fishing Bridge, an outlet of Yellowstone Lake, a wide variety of animal and birdlife can be observed – fishing, however, is not permitted!

One of the Park's most visited features, the powerful Yellowstone River plummets a total of 417 feet in two spectacular falls. These are the 109-foot cascade of the Upper Falls (right) and the thundering Lower Falls (facing page and overleaf), twice the height of Niagara. Below: viewed from Inspiration Point – one of many observation sites accessible via nearby roads and trails – Yellowstone River is dwarfed by its looming, forest-covered canyon. Formed during the ice ages, it was the 24 miles of this twisting, 1,200-foot-deep canyon, with its sheer, red and yellow-colored rock walls, which first inspired Indians and early explorers to name the canyon and its river, Yellowstone.

Below: Kepler Cascades of the fast-flowing Firehole River. Facing page top: Scaup Lake, fringed by snow-laden firs. Even in June, snow lies deep in the mountain forests of Yellowstone (facing page bottom) and total snowfall in some places can exceed 300 inches. Overleaf: a winter view of the Lower Falls, seen from Lookout Point.

Yellowstone, with its unique and varied landscape, is a haven for wildlife. Forests of aspen (facing page top) and lodgepole pine (facing page bottom), like the woodlands near Bridge Bay (below), provide welcome shade and cover. Top right: the Hayden Valley with its broad, curving channels and open banks and the Gallatin River Valley (right), support large herds of elk and bison. Underground heat causes snow to melt, replenishing the many water sources crucial for the animals' survival. These include the Madison (bottom right) and the Gibbon rivers (overleaf). Above: Kepler Rapids.

Yellowstone still draws many visitors during the winter months, when the thermal features are often even more spectacular. Snow-covered Morning Glory Pool (below) and Old Faithful Geyser (facing page top) – two atttractions at Upper Geyser Basin. Facing page center: West Thumb Geyser Basin and (facing page bottom), bison at Opalescent Pool, Black Sand Basin. Animals gather in geyser basins in search of food, as the warm ground reduces snow cover and promotes growth of some grasses and mosses. Despite the thermal features, air temperatures can fall to –76°F. Overleaf: the Upper Falls of theYellowstone River.

Yellowstone is a place of infinite beauty, variety and dramatic scenery. Below: the distinctive silhouette of Castle Geyser's geyserite cone. Facing page: breathtaking sunsets over Porcelain Basin (top), the Firehole River (bottom) and over Old Faithful (overleaf). A fine view of Clepsydra Geyser (last page), Lower Geyser Basin. This feature is easily accessible from the Fountain Paint Pot Nature Trail.